CONTENTS

YOUTUBE FOR REAL ESTATE AGENTS

Learn how to get free real estate leads and never cold call again

by Karin Carr

Disclaimer

*Although the author has made every effort to ensure that the
information in this book is correct at the time of publication, the
author does not assume any liability to any part of loss, damage,
or disruption caused by this book. The author is not responsible
for any results obtained or not obtained by implementing a
YouTube strategy. The advice and strategies contained herein
may or may not be suitable for your business and situation. The
reader of this publication assumes all responsibility for the use
of these materials, the advice given, and the actions taken.*

FOREWORD

I met Karin Carr through my mastermind program, Traffic & Leads Masters. She came to me with an already wildly successful system that was helping real estate agents all over the country, and she needed a little help getting her message out to even more. I haven't known Karin for more than a year or two, but from the moment I met her and learned about her powerful method, it was clear to me she had something special.

Throughout my 13+ years in digital marketing, I've had the pleasure of working with many real estate agents. I've helped multiple agents build websites, rank on search engines, buy media, and work with the multiple listing services to get their name out there so they can find more clients and grow their businesses. I've learned one thing from my work in the real estate industry: 90% of what will determine your success is based on how effective your marketing is. The individuals that have nailed their marketing and stood out from their competitors are the winners.

Most folks in real estate say and do the exact same things to market themselves. They end up being a commodity. They all market their services the same way, say the same things, and have a really difficult time standing out. The answer to not being a commodity is to find your audience of potential clients (or allow them to find you) and learn how to connect with them so they will "feel" compelled to take action and call you.

Nothing is more powerful at doing this than utilizing the world's second largest search engine: YouTube. Your potential clients are there searching, and nothing is more powerful at creating intimacy, trust, and connection than video. This, my friends, is lightning in a bottle. It's the perfect mix of audience and connection that has seasoned digital marketers, like myself, extremely excited.

In Karin Carr's powerful book, YouTube for Real Estate Agents, she outlines the perfect formula for both finding and connecting with your audience. The principles in this book are tried and true digital marketing tactics that will work for anyone in the real estate industry that is ready to simply follow the steps.

Over the years, I've run into many marketing gurus peddling the next best thing to those in real estate because they are an easy target. The real estate industry is highly competitive, and the participants are always looking for the best way to get ahead of their competitors. Here is where Karin and her formula are different. Unlike many of those simply peddling the "answer" to more leads for your real estate business, Karin is a REALTOR® herself. She started in Savannah in June 2017 with no sphere of influence, no clients, no name recognition, and definitely no market share. As of the writing of this foreword, she has over 200,000 views and 4,000 subscribers to her YouTube channel.

She's been there, done that. Karin has detailed her experience into a book revealing the exact steps she employed on her journey to becoming a highly successful real estate agent in a matter of months! Not only has she been successful with this process, but I have seen others implement the strategies and grow their businesses as well. This formula is legit.

This book outlines everything you need to know to NEVER make another cold call and to become wildly successful in the real estate industry. Karin even covers the very intense topic of mindset. Conquering a fear of being on camera will hold back many real estate agents from employing the strategies in this book, but Karin addresses this challenge in a highly effective way.

The bottom line is, if you've picked up this book, you did it for a reason. It means you're ready. You're ready to take your real estate business to the next level. So here it is. It's all right here in this amazing book. Go employ this powerful system that Karin has outlined, sit back, and watch the leads roll in.

One-Click Lindsey Anderson
President & CEO of Traffic & Leads

INTRODUCTION

H ello, my fellow real estate video marketing genius! Oh wait—you aren't a genius quite yet? Keep reading this book and I promise, soon you will know so much more than your competition, you'll be a genius in no time.

Congratulations on taking the first step to never having to buy another real estate lead again. Sounds pretty good, doesn't it? I am so excited you have decided to join me on this YouTube journey! Right now, as I write this, I am sitting here with a big, stupid grin on my face because I know something you don't know. I know your career is about to change—quite possibly explode—if you go all in on your YouTube channel.

Let me tell you a story about Cheryl.

Cheryl has been a real estate agent for several years, and she's good at what she does, but she hates the grind of constant lead generation. She doesn't really like calling her sphere to beg for referrals and absolutely detests cold calling, so she avoids it like the plague. As a result, her business is on a constant roller coaster. One month, she has two or three closings, then she has none for the next three months.

She tried running Facebook ads, and yes, she got a lot of leads, but the conversion rate was abysmal. She considered buying leads from the big portals, but they're so expensive and they want her to commit to an entire year. Her financial situation is always a source of stress because she never knows how much money she can expect to make each month. She never sets money aside for taxes because she needs every penny of that commission check, and come tax time, she's a nervous wreck, worrying how much she'll owe.

One day her husband says he's been offered a job in another city. Relocating will mean many new opportunities for them so they decide to go for it, even though she knows starting over in a new city will be hard. Cheryl has been blogging occasionally for the last year, and it has started to pay off. Prospects find her online, and even though the leads trickle in, they are usually pretty good leads that convert easily. The blog posts with videos in them seem to do the best so she puts the videos on YouTube as well.

Right after she moves to her new town, she gets an amazing phone call! Someone found her YouTube channel, watched all her videos, and decided they want her to help them buy a house. Unfortunately, it was in her old market, which is now all the way across the state. So, she refers them to one of her former colleagues, but this gets her thinking. They felt like they knew her already after watching so many of her videos, so she decides she will commit to making weekly YouTube videos. She promises herself she will give it at least six months and see what happens.

Cheryl spends the first few months learning her way around her new market, taking pictures, touring different neighborhoods, and taking video of the local landmarks and hotspots. She uses this footage to make videos telling people how great this place is. She also makes videos about more general real estate topics, such as what a VA loan is, how to know when you're ready to buy your first house, or how to stage your home when it's for sale.

After a few months, Cheryl hits the motherlode! A couple in town is planning to move to Florida. They saw her YouTube videos and call her to make an appointment to discuss selling their home. Cheryl arrives at their house one Saturday morning prepared to win this listing at all costs, armed with answers to overcome all their objections. After all, she has only lived here for three months and hasn't sold any houses in their neighborhood, so she assumes they will bring up those objections.

Instead, they sign the listing agreement on the spot. This couple had already decided to hire her when they called her! They loved her immediately and didn't argue when she tells them what she charges. The best part is that they didn't even interview anyone else!

A few weeks later, Cheryl gets another phone call. This is from another seller, and it's a similar situation. The next lead is from a buyer looking to relocate to her city. He has accepted a job offer in town and has to be there in five weeks. He needs to find a house pronto!

Within six months, Cheryl is getting a steady stream of inbound leads that didn't cost her a dime. She also starts receiving referrals from other agents around the country. This is amazing! She knows agents spending thousands of dollars a month to buy leads from the big portals, or they spend that much on Pay-Per-Click (PPC) and Facebook ads to get leads that take forever to convert. She tells everyone how great YouTube is, but they simply smile and nod, then go back to writing big fat checks to their lead sources.

After a year, Cheryl hires a virtual assistant, then another one, then a showing assistant who later becomes a buyer's agent, then another buyer's agent, and finally begins looking to hire a listing specialist. She has gone from being a total unknown in her market to being a team leader.

She is earning a great income while working fewer hours than she ever has since she got her real estate license. No more marathon showings on Saturdays and no more spending hours a day in the car. And she has been in her new city for only two years.

Not too shabby, huh?

My name is Karin Carr. I am a REALTOR® in Savannah, Georgia. As you can probably guess, that is my personal story, and it's 100% true. Cheryl is actually my sister's name, and I stole it for the purpose of this story. Thanks, sis!

I started blogging when I lived in the Atlanta metro area, and I read somewhere that if you embed a YouTube video in your blog post it was something like 43 times more likely to rank on the first page of Google search results. That's crazy that something so simple could have such a HUGE impact.

In the beginning, I started making videos only to make the blog post rank higher. I used YouTube as a repository for the videos so that I could embed the link in the blog. It never occurred to me that people were looking for this information on YouTube. Or that my videos themselves would show up on the first page of Google search results. Not only the blog post, but also the actual video.

What happened after we relocated to Savannah was nothing short of miraculous. My business literally blew up. I was getting calls, emails, and Facebook messages several times a day from other agents asking me questions about using YouTube. I was asked to speak at conventions about video marketing.

After about a year, I began teaching agents across the world how to do this for themselves. I created a training program called YouTube for Agents so that I could share what was working for me with anyone who wanted step by step instruction. I am a teacher at heart, and I love sharing what works so that others can have the same success in their own markets. Nothing makes me happier than hearing my students' success stories!

My goal is to help you kick your self-limiting beliefs to the curb and create the business you want and the income you deserve, all without working eighteen-hour days to get there.

I wrote this book because anyone can do what I'm doing if they will simply do it. I'm not better on camera than anyone else. Sure, I have my own quirky personality but so do you. I'm not younger, I'm not prettier, I'm not skinnier, I'm not better trained, and I certainly don't have better equipment. Anybody can do what I have done and achieve similar results.

You might think no one would want to watch you on YouTube because you're too old, too overweight, or too insert your silly excuse here. I've heard everything from, "I have no idea what to say, and no one would want to watch my videos anyway," to "My voice is so damned annoying I can't even stand to listen to myself!" I'm here to tell you it's not true. Do you have friends? Do you have clients? Then people don't hate the sound of your voice. And you only think you have nothing to say because you have no idea what consumers find interesting. Well, we're going to fix that with this challenge!

Generating business doesn't have to be hard. Attracting new clients on a weekly or even daily basis doesn't have to be difficult or expensive. It's not a mystery, and I'm going to tell you exactly how to get started.

Before you go thinking that this is going to be a ton of work, I want to clarify something.

> *I am emphatically anti-hustle. I do not believe for one minute you need to work eighteen-hour days in order to make a great living.*

I hate those grind and hustle memes I see all over social media. You know the ones I'm talking about. Getting up at 5 am and working untill 11 pm is not something we should aspire to. You need a life and I bet your family would like to see you once in a while.

You also do not need to have a videographer follow you around all day with a camera to be successful. If you have the money to do that, more power to you. I sure would love that! And if you do, your videos will look much cooler and a lot more polished. But it's absolutely not necessary to kill it on YouTube.

I believe with my whole heart that no matter what your platform of choice is, if you commit to mastering that particular platform, you will be successful. Mine is YouTube, and I will do my damnedest to convince you by the end of this challenge why it should be yours too!

Over the next seven days, I will give you daily assignments. You will read a chapter in this book, take action, and get it done. And then, you'll move on to the next task. The more of these tasks you complete, the better the results you'll start to see ... and they'll keep growing the more consistent you are.

> *In a nutshell, I'm here to help you get your butt in gear! Stop making excuses and just freaking do it already.*

You will be tempted to skip the tasks that seem like too much work. Don't do it. Everything I tell you to do is 100% necessary if you want to have the kind of business I'm talking about. If it takes you more than a day, that's fine. If it takes four days because you were really busy or went on vacation, that's ok. I get it, we're busy people. But be sure to complete a task before moving onto the next step. Trust me, you will get so much more out of this challenge if you do all these steps in order.

By the time you complete the challenge, you'll have a YouTube channel that is set up to become a client magnet. All that will be left is for you to start making regular content to put on the You-Tube channel. If you commit to doing this, the change you will see in your business will absolutely amaze you.

Sounds too good to be true, doesn't it? Well, there is one slight catch, hardly worth even mentioning really. And it goes like this —*if you don't create the content, if you don't create valuable videos, you will not get new clients.*

You cannot expect to make one video that will go viral and get 1,000,000 views, which will bring you enough business for the next four years. It ain't gonna happen. You must put out consistent content for your channel to take off. So, don't spend all this time making a great channel and then fail to keep making videos. I have built my business on making one video a week. That's it. Not daily vlogging, not Facebook Lives three times a week. One video a week, period.

I promise you, YouTube can be the best free lead gen strategy you will ever find. It's fun, it's cost-effective (free), and it's a great use of your time. A few hours spent creating a video can bring you business for years to come. Notice I'm not just saying leads but prospects who call you and sign an exclusive agreement to work with you, then buy or sell a house, and you get paid at the end of the day.

How would you like to get results like these?

I just got another lead today from a lady who is moving from San Francisco and wants to buy a home for her son for $800k CASH, and then after she buys her son a house she wants to buy a house for herself. I am telling you, these

types of videos work!!!!! - Angela

I am still new to real estate so I needed a low (or no cost) way to generate leads. We closed our first YouTube lead in April 2019 and since then we've closed an additional 4, and have 1 more in the pipeline. - Lindsay

Refocused on YouTube after getting sidetracked - just put a $905k buyer under contract yesterday. - Cyndee

One last thing. If you see a link in this book followed by an asterisk (*), that means it's an affiliate link. I don't have a lot of them, and I only recommend solutions/products that I actually own and use myself. If you click the link and end up purchasing whatever I was recommending, it's at no additional cost to you, and I will receive a small commission. Passive income is an amazing thing.

YOUTUBER, IT'S TIME TO TAKE ACTION!

Answer these questions:

What made you pick up this book?

What are you hoping will change in your business by having a great YouTube presence?

If you knew it would bring you one or two additional closings a month, would you commit to creating YouTube content?

Would you dedicate half an hour a day (that's only 3-4 hours a week once you get the hang of it and pass the initial learning curve) to make six figures a year without spending money on ads or buying leads?

What activities could you give up in order to make time for creating YouTube content? It could be cold calling or door knocking. Or it could be not watching the Game of Thrones marathon this weekend. We all have the same amount of hours in the day. How you spend them is up to you. Just sayin'...

How would it feel knowing you never had to call total strangers to beg for business again?

How would your business, indeed, your life change?

How would your financial situation change?

If you no longer had to grind for two to four hours a day generating leads, how would that change your quality of life? Would you have more time to spend with your family?

Would you have more time to take care of yourself so you aren't always so stressed? This business can be stressful and you deserve downtime.

When do you plan to complete the daily challenge tasks? Be specific. Choose a time of day when you will sit down, open this book, and do the work required. What time works best for you to do it? I'd allow 30 - 45 minutes a day.

I want you to put it on your calendar. Set an appointment that you will not change. This is strategic business development. It is an important strategy for growing your business, and you should treat this time as such.

DAY ONE: YOUR ICA - IDEAL CLIENT AVATAR

This is an extremely important step most people skip right over when they start a YouTube channel or any sort of content marketing strategy for that matter. But you're not going to skip this step because you are way better than most agents who try something for three days and then give up. And the very fact you are reading this book means you actually want to do this the right way.

Most REALTORS® think they should work with anyone who wants to buy or sell any type of home in a thirty-mile radius. They need the business, so they're willing to work with anyone and everyone.

Hear me and hear me well—your ideal client is not anyone who can fog a mirror! That is way too broad. By being more intentional about the types of clients you want to attract, you practically guarantee those exact clients will be able to find you.

Do you want to be known as just another real estate agent in your area? Or do you want to be known as the go-to agent who caters to (insert your specialty here)?

Let's play a game. In an ideal world, if you had so many leads coming in that you could pick and choose who you wanted to work with, who would that be? Now, I'm not talking about discrimination or violating fair housing laws. I'm not advocating that you refuse to work with any protected classes of people, so don't get your panties in a wad.

> *What I am talking about is narrowing down your marketing so that you attract clients that are perfect for you. You can do that by the content you create and by the personality you show on camera.*

The smaller your channel, the more necessary it is to niche down. It is not just recommended, it is *mandatory* if you want to be seen as an authority.

Most people see REALTORS® as being interchangeable. They don't see us as having any significant value over the real estate agent next door. And everybody has an Uncle Joe or a cousin Sue with a real estate license. We're all simply door openers, right? (Ha! Little do they know!)

So, what can you do to differentiate yourself and show your value? You do that by being a specialist. *I don't care what you specialize in, but you must specialize in something.*

Your specialty could be a type of client (empty nesters or first-time buyers, for example). It could be dog lovers, soccer moms, or parents with preschoolers who want to buy in a certain school district. It could be single professional women or urban professionals who want to buy their first investment property. Again, you are not saying you will only work with these people. These are merely the types of people you really enjoy working with, so you'd like to help more clients like this.

Here's an example. I love working with seniors. I've had many clients buy a house in the town where their grandkids live. They want to be able to see their children and grandchildren a lot more often, and it's usually a really fun transaction because they have such a good time during the process.

They end up adopting me, and usually my husband and kids too, into their family. After they move in, they have us over for pool parties. I love working with these people! And the fact that they have money to spend usually makes for a smoother transaction too. They're financially stable so their loan doesn't get denied at the 11th hour. In fact, they often pay cash, and since they have bought and sold many houses in their lives, they don't freak out over every little detail. I don't have to tell you that when the transaction is less stressful it's a lot more enjoyable for everyone involved.

> *Would it be okay for me to say that seniors are my ideal customer avatar? Of course! I'm not refusing to work with anyone under the age of 55; I'm simply intending to attract that specific demographic with the content I create.*

Your niche could be a type of transaction—probate sales, REO listings, or people who are forced to sell their home because they're getting divorced. New construction and pre builds is another profitable niche if you have a lot of construction going on in your area.

It can be a geographic farm area, whether that's a town, a zip code, or a subdivision. Be sure there's enough business in that farm area to keep you busy. A subdivision with 100 houses where only 12 homes a year turnover is not going to be big enough to sustain you.

Another great niche is people with certain jobs—people in the military, schoolteachers, doctors, or first responders. If you were a nurse before you went into real estate, maybe you could specialize in working with nurses. I'm going to go out on a limb here and say you probably like working with people like you, so let's try to attract people like you!

It can be types of properties—tiny homes, condos, homes on the water, log cabins, beachfront, or penthouses in the city. When I moved to Savannah, I decided my niche was going to be military. My husband is retired from the Air Force, so we shop on base at the commissary, fly on military aircrafts when we go on vacation, and stay in military hotels when we travel. We are a military family, and I love working with military buyers and sellers.

The first videos I made were focused on issues specific to military members. Are you PCS'ing to Hunter Army Airfield? Do you know how to use your VA entitlement to buy a house? Can your Base Allowance for Housing (BAH) cover your mortgage payment? How do you find a house all the way across the world when you get orders to transfer somewhere new? If you have to sell quickly because you have to report to your new duty station in 60 days, how do you do that?

I made videos to appeal to this specific niche. Did that mean I didn't receive any other leads besides military buyers? Heck no! In fact, the first lead I got was from someone who had no military ties whatsoever. The second lead I got was a military seller, not a military buyer.

In other words, you won't automatically alienate people who do not fit your ideal client avatar. By having a very specific niche, it makes it so much easier to decide what you're going to talk about.

Because you know exactly who you are speaking to, you then know what issues are important to them.

Nowadays, most of my YouTube leads are people moving to Savannah, military or not. I have accidentally become a relocation specialist. But I like this niche, so when it started happening, I ran with it.

Hi Karin,
My husband and I found you on youtube. Currently, we are located in South Korea, my husband is active duty with the army. We will be locating to the hunter army base in September. My children and I plan on returning back to the states by June to begin our search for a home. We have a trusted lender already who let us know we qualify for 200k. We are first home buyers. We have looked at several realtors and have enjoyed your youtube videos the most. We understand being in Korea kind of makes it difficult and maybe pointless to contact you, but with being first-time buyers we are not sure how to start the process other than sticking our hands out there and trying to become acquainted with a realtor and the homes we truly want. I was wondering if you are willing to start working with us and maybe really help us narrow down our choices and our firm deal breakers when it comes to home buying? I understand working through email may be difficult and I apologize for the inconvenience if you feel its too early to start looking we understand and appreciate your time! Thank you

On Aug 15, 2019, at 8:27 PM, ███████████████ wrote:

Karin,

I saw your youtube videos on "Moving to Savannah" and "Love/Hate Living in Savannah." My husband and I are considering moving to Savannah to be closer to his off-shore job. We are from Washington State and currently have our house on the market. I thought I'd send you this email as inquiry to any rental offerings or rental agencies you would recommend as we'd love to rent before settling in on buying a home in the area. We have two Golden Retrievers that are apart of the family and are wondering how difficult it may be to rent with the dogs. By the way, great job on the videos! I do marketing videos myself and would hope I could easily find a job there.

Message

I am interested in ██████████ Savannah, GA 31404 . Hello! I am sitting on a job offer at the Memorial Hospital. I am currently in Phoenix and would love to find out about this home. I would relocate by 9/25.

Figure 1.1 Examples of leads I have gotten recently by niche marketing on YouTube

Back during the crash, I lived in northern California and I specialized in bank-foreclosed listings. In 2008, I closed 72 transaction sides all by myself with no team, and almost every single one of them was an REO listing. The best years I've ever had in my business have been when I had a very clearly-defined specialty.

I know it's really scary to niche down when you desperately need business, but I'm telling you this is the secret to higher volume!

You have to figure out who you want to work with, who you would enjoy working with, and it must be a niche that would give you enough business to give you the volume and income you desire.

Please listen to me—you're not limiting yourself by having a niche. You are focusing your marketing message so that the right people hear it.

The students in my YouTube for Agents program that rake in the most leads all have a clearly defined niche—new construction, investors, specific neighborhoods, horse properties, seniors who are downsizing, probate sales, or they followed my example and became relocation specialists too.

You're not excluding people by having a specialty. You are establishing yourself as the local expert and as a result you draw your ideal people to you. So, don't be greedy. Don't think you have to work with everybody. There is plenty of business to go around.

You also don't have to work with people you don't like. Yes, that's right! I am giving you permission to reject the clients who are jerks. You do not have to be a doormat, and you don't have to jump every time an unreasonable client snaps their fingers. You get to decide who you want to work with and who you don't.

Let that soak in ... you get to decide if you want to take someone on as a client. You don't have to work with every single person that crosses your path simply because you really need the money. That sounds pretty fantastic, don't you think?

If you try to be all things to all people, you are so bland that people don't care enough to get to know you, let alone like and trust you. And if you say, "I'm going to specialize in first time buyers, seniors who are downsizing, and luxury properties," that's like trying to chase three dogs at the same time, and they're all running in different directions. Call me crazy, but I don't think that's going to be very effective.

Instead I want you to think, "Who can I serve the easiest? Who can I speak to with the most authority? Who can I deliver the most value to? Who can I help the most because I understand them and their problems? "

And usually, that's people like you. It doesn't have to be, but it's certainly easier if you have been in their shoes before.

You will also attract people who genuinely like your personality. Which means you have to be yourself on camera. Don't wear a suit if you normally wear shorts and aloha shirts. Don't try to be professional and straight faced if you normally joke around a lot with clients. Look professional and don't be a slob, but it's ok to be yourself.

This is by far my favorite aspect of lead generation on YouTube. When you are yourself on camera, you will attract people who have similar personalities as you. Like attracts like.

When I first started making videos, I never stopped to think about that. I was only hoping that someone, anyone, would contact me. If you've watched my videos, you know I am pretty goofy. I make lots of jokes, I talk in silly voices, and I laugh a lot. I make parodies, and sometimes I even dress up as different characters.

I've taken the DISC profile assessment (https://www.discprofile.com/what-is-disc/overview/) and I am a High I (someone who likes to talk. A LOT.) I don't attract a lot of High Cs, the very analytical people, the people that want the graphs, statistics, and data. That's so not me. Therefore, the High Cs don't really call me all that frequently, and I am totally ok with it.

When they want to know all the data and I don't immediately have all those statistics at my fingertips, it stresses me out. I think, *"Oh no, what if I say the wrong thing? What if I give them the wrong information? What if they buy an investment property based on my recommendation, but I gave them the wrong cap rate, and now they're pissed off, and they sue me? I'll lose my license, go broke, and I'll have to work at McDonalds!"*

Instead, I like to work with people who are more into how the house makes them feel versus the people who want the cold hard data. And I naturally attract those people by the way I show up on camera.

I get a lot of phone calls from people who say things like, "Girl, I feel like I know you already. We're going to be BFFs. When I move to Savannah and buy my house, you're coming over for margaritas, and we're going to have one helluva pool party!"

These people don't try to talk me down on my commission when I show up to list their house because they already know, like, and trust me and they see my value. I've become really, really good friends with some of these clients, because when I am being myself on camera, they feel like they know me personally. When we finally meet for the first time, they hug me. I've had people bring me coffee or gifts! It doesn't feel like I've never met them before; it feels like we're old friends.

Here's an email I got from a prospect who not only became a client and bought a house, she also ended up writing guest blog posts for my web site later down the road.

> *Hello Karin, our family is planning to relocate to Savannah, GA via Nashville, TN in the next year or two. We have vacationed on Tybee Island 3 times in the past 6 years and adore the City of Savannah. After our most recent trip, we decided to make Savannah our permanent home. In researching the area, I stumbled upon your YouTube channel. I commend you on your exceptional use of social media marketing, you really grabbed my attention. Finding a great realtor is difficult, but after watching a few of your videos, I felt we could work together nicely. Your personality is quirky...as is mine.*

This client signed an exclusive agreement to work with me before we ever even met. She built a house here, and we have become good friends. When you adore your clients and they feel the same way about you, it's a pretty fantastic business model.

◆ ◆ ◆

YOUTUBER ACTION ITEM #1

Your homework assignment for tonight is to brainstorm some niches. To help you create your ideal client avatar, I've created a worksheet for you to download as a special bonus.

Download my Ideal Client Avatar worksheet here:
https://www.youtubesuccesschecklist.com/ica/

You are not only going to choose your ideal client, you're going to actively repel the people you would not enjoy working with. And that's not only ok, that's also desirable!

Let's say you do videos where you are specifically talking to dog lovers. Does that mean you will never get a lead from someone who doesn't have a dog? No, of course not. You will probably get plenty of them. You might turn off some of the cat people. And you will definitely turn off the people who hate dogs.

Is that ok? Yes! Because if you have a fur baby you dote on, do you really want a client who thinks dogs are awful, hateful creatures? Would you ever want to work with someone who thinks it's ok to physically mistreat an animal? Would you really kick your values to the curb for the sake of a paycheck? Lord, I hope not.

> *I might be beating a dead horse here but this is the part that most agents tend to struggle with the most at the beginning. So I'm really trying to make sure you understand that having a specialty is the way to go on YouTube.*

So, tonight we're going to pick out your niche. Think of past clients you have loved working with. What were they like? Did they buy certain types of homes? Were they in certain areas?

You want to pick niches you would enjoy working with, not only profitable niches. Life is too short to go to work every day hating your job and representing people who are jerks.

So, brainstorm your niches. Come up with as many ideas as you like but then narrow it down to no more than three niches. See if one jumps out at you or whether you would be happier servicing one niche more than the others. Would one niche give you more business than the others? Can you combine them? Such as downsizing seniors who are cat lovers? If so, great!

Once you have determined your niche, now you're going to imagine the actual client who represents this niche. This is your ideal client avatar. I want you to really flesh out who this person is. Give him or her a name, an age, what they do for a living, how much money they make, whether they want to buy or sell, where they live and want to live, if they have kids or grandkids, if they have pets, etc.

Here's a sample ideal client avatar:

Carla is a single woman who's thirty-seven. She's never been married and has never bought a home before because she didn't think she could do it on a solo income. She's not handy and doesn't know how to fix things and figured renting was easier. But she is tired of flushing her rent money down the toilet and having nothing to show for it.

Carla makes a decent salary as a teacher, $40,000 a year, so she wants to buy her first home. She thinks a condo or townhouse would be ideal so she wouldn't have to do any yard maintenance. Carla is 5'7", has brown hair and green eyes. She has a cat named Chester. She is a doting aunt to her three nieces and nephews but doesn't have kids of her own unless you count Chester.

She teaches sixth grade at Middleton Elementary School in Sommersville.

(You can even print out a photo you find on the internet of your Carla. Tape it up on the wall or next to your camera when you're recording so you remember exactly who you're talking to.)

Can you see how knowing exactly who you want to attract will help you be able to come up with video topics more easily? If you know her challenges and obstacles to homeownership, now you are in the perfect position to be able to help her!

You will come up with great ideas for video topics, and when you record your videos, the women who watch them are going to feel like you are speaking directly to them. Which you are!

It makes your job as a content creator much easier, and it focuses your marketing message like a laser beam to the person who is perfectly ready to hear it. (If you are newly licensed and don't have a lot of transactions under your belt, that's ok! You can still come up with a specialty—it will just be based on your desires rather than on past experience.)

DAY TWO: SCOPE OUT YOUR COMPETITION

Welcome back to Day Two of the YouTube challenge! How did last night's assignment go? I am curious to know what you thought about niching down. Was it scary? Did you feel like you were turning away business by picking a niche? Or did it make you excited because now you have a roadmap for success? Because make no mistake, that's what this is.

I recently did this challenge live on Facebook in my group, YouTube for Real Estate Agents – https://www.facebook.com/groups/YouTubeforrealestateagents/. On Day Two when I asked this question, people said it was really hard. They were afraid to niche down, or they said things like: "My niche is military buyers, seniors downsizing, my farm neighborhood, and beach homes." Does that sound like a niche to you? No, that's four different niches.

If someone arrives at your YouTube channel and can't tell what the heck your channel is about, will they subscribe? That's a big, fat no.

As I said yesterday on Day One, being a specialist is the best way to stand out in a sea of real estate agents. Everyone sells houses, everyone says they look out for their clients' best interests, everyone says they're honest and trustworthy and available and they have great reviews, blah blah blah… everyone says the same thing.

Being a specialist is the only way you can differentiate yourself. And the smaller your channel, the more important it is to have a specialty. You won't reach everyone in your market, but you don't need to. By focusing down on a specific type of client, you are guaranteeing that client can find you without spending hours researching real estate agents in their area.

When you niche down, your videos act like a magnet. They pull your ideal clients to you. You are going to be the perfect resource for your niche, community, and market. And I am willing to bet that very few other agents in your market are doing anything like this. When there's no competition, it's really easy to dominate your market!

My college roommate was the homecoming queen at her high school her senior year. There were 11 people in her senior class and only five were girls. She always joked that it wasn't too hard to be voted homecoming queen when you only had four other girls to compete against!

That's how it was for me and will most likely be for you too. Very few people are doing any sort of video marketing consistently, and even fewer are on YouTube. And of the ones that are, how many are in your exact niche, in your same market area, and are getting tons of business because they're doing it the right way like you soon will be?

<<Insert the sound of crickets chirping>>

In today's challenge, we're going to scope out your competition. Let's see who you're up against. I bet you're going to be really happy with what you discover!

When I did this exercise after deciding to make YouTube my platform of choice, I was thrilled at how little competition there was! Savannah has a population of about 150,000 in the city and 300,000 in the entire metro area. It's big, but it's not huge.

Now, if you are in a large city, you might have more competition. Or you might have one or two agents who are really going for it on YouTube. That's ok, no need to freak out. You are operating from a place of abundance, not scarcity. There is more than enough business to go around, and you do not need 100% market share to make a fantastic living.

First, make sure you are *not logged into Google* and go open up You-Tube. You can open an incognito window if you're using Chrome so you get truly accurate results. We don't want the search results to show you things based on your past search history, your IP address, or any cookies. We're going to see what kind of competition you will have in your market.

Let's say you live in Boise, Idaho. Type things into the search bar such as:

> *Boise real estate*
> *Boise REALTOR*
> *Boise real estate agents*
> *Real estate agents in Boise*
> *Homes for sale in Boise*
> *Best neighborhoods in Boise*
> *Moving to Boise*
> *Real estate agents in Boise using video*

Check out the videos that show up. Are they made by the same person over and over again? How many views do those videos have? Watch a few and see what the video content is like.

Is it interesting? Is it evergreen content? (Evergreen content is a topic that will be relevant years from now. A new listing is not evergreen content, because as soon as the property sells, it's no longer relevant.) Are most of the videos listing tours? How old are the videos? Are there any good videos that are a month old or are they very generic videos that are a few years old?

By generic, I mean it's a video of your area with stock footage set to music, or even worse, those cartoon explainer videos. They are nothing more than commercials. The agent is not on camera talking. There's no opportunity to connect with the agent because he or she is not on screen except for their business card information at the very end that says, "Everything I touch turns to sold!" You know the videos I'm talking about. (If that's your tag line and I offended you... sorry, not sorry. I really hate that tag line.)

Don't panic if you see other agents making videos. They might be doing it, but they are probably not doing it effectively. Or they might have a totally different niche than you, if they even have one at all. If you live in an area with a guy who specializes in selling condos and you want to specialize in selling lakefront homes, there is plenty of room for both of you to be YouTubers and to both make a killing in business.

Back when I did this exercise after moving to Savannah, there was only one agent in my market who seemed to have any YouTube presence whatsoever. He was making videos pretty consistently about really good topics. They weren't well produced, didn't have lots of slick graphics, and he wasn't terribly exciting on camera (at least in my opinion) but the content was good.

His YouTube channel had four subscribers. Four. Each video was lucky to get fifteen views. Every now and then, he had a video that had 100 views, and it was probably because he had run an ad. He's up to eight subscribers now, two years later. <<*Sad emoji face*>> (No, not really. I'm laughing all the way to the bank!)

It probably sounds really cocky to say this, but I didn't consider him to be competition. I mean, come on! He gets twelve views on a video. How hard is it to beat that? You can get probably twelve views just by asking your friends and family members to watch your video.

> *The moral of the story? You can make the best content in the world, but if no one sees it, it will never bring you any business. So, if you come across agents that are actually making videos, don't panic—rejoice! You're going to leave them in the dust.*

Usually when my students do this exercise, they see a whole bunch of generic listing videos. A virtual tour where there is no agent on camera, no voiceover, and it's a two-year-old video to boot. So again... no competition.

YOUTUBER ACTION ITEM #2

Your assignment is to scope out your competition and see how many people in your market are actively using YouTube as a lead generation strategy. Jot down what you found doing your research.

Who is doing video well in your area? Anyone? If not, this is a wide-open playing field, and you will soon dominate it!

If there is someone, what makes their videos good? Are they charismatic on camera? Are they enjoyable to watch? Are they interesting? Or are they simply the only game in town?

Do an honest review of some of their videos and see if there are things you could do better. See if there are any videos they did that were ok but not detailed, not thorough, or maybe they were just boring as hell. Could you make a video on that subject but make it a lot more interesting?

No matter whether you find tons of competition or none at all, there is plenty of opportunity for you. Because you will soon know the secret sauce to getting your videos found. Which brings me to Day Three...

DAY THREE: THE SECRET SAUCE - SEO

So ... did you find out that you have some competition yesterday? Or did you realize the YouTube playing field is wide open?

Regardless of what you discovered, please remember that even if other people are making videos in your area, there is still tons of opportunity for you to start getting business from this platform. I could have exactly the same niche as someone else in my market. We could be targeting the same clients. But if I'm a goofball girl and he's a very serious data driven man, we will attract different clients. And as I said before, that's a good thing.

Get ready because this is an exciting day! This is how I've been able generate so many leads, clients, and closings. This is how my students are doing it, whether they live in a huge city like Phoenix or Toronto. or a small town in Ohio.

When I did this challenge live on Facebook the first time, I had a few hundred people register to attend. And the day we tackled this topic, people said things like, "OMG! Mind blown!" Or, "Holy $#@! I had no idea... this is seriously magic."

Prepare to be dazzled and amazed, my friend.

We identified what your niches would be on Day One, and after doing some recon on the competition, you know where there are holes to be filled. Today, we're going to start coming up with video subject ideas and learn how to do research to ensure that those videos are going to get found—and seen.

Let's say you have an idea in mind for a video, and you're gung-ho to go film it. You wake up, do your hair, dress nicely, and set up your camera, lights, and microphone. Whoa, whoa, whoa there! Don't you dare press record until you <<insert dramatic music here>> do your keyword research.

> *Keyword research is simply doing some investigation to see what people are typing into the YouTube or Google search bars. I'm sure you already know that Google owns YouTube, right? And YouTube is just another search engine, which happens to be the second biggest search engine in the world. And it's owned by the #1 search engine. So does it make sense to make the search engine happy when you're creating content? Why yes, yes it does!*

Back to my example about what people are typing into the search bars, either on YouTube or Google. Are they typing in "How much does it cost to sell a house?" Or are they typing "Cost to sell a house?" It's the same subject, but the words you use are the difference between that video getting you hundreds or even thousands of views and a bunch of listings in the coming year, or showing up on the 7th page of search results.

Keyword research is truly miraculous! It allows you to find out exactly which videos will get the most views before you even make the video.

You are using Search Engine Optimization (SEO) to optimize your video for the search engines so that Google and YouTube will rank your video higher than your competitors' videos.

Here is my favorite super cheap tool for doing keyword research. (Are you seeing a theme here? I'm all about free and/or cheap stuff.) This little piece of software is the coolest thing ever, and if you have followed me for a while, you have heard me talk about this ad nauseum.

It's called Keywords Everywhere. Go to https://keywordseverywhere.com/ and get their very inexpensive plugin. (As of the time of this writing it's $10 for 100,000 credits. I expect that to last me at least six months.) It's available for both Chrome and Firefox.

Once you install Keywords Everywhere, something magical happens—it shows you how much search volume there is for the exact phrase someone types into the Google search bar. (Mind blown, right?)

Let's use an example of "moving to Nashville." Go to Google and type that phrase into the search bar. Assuming that you have already installed Keywords Everywhere, here's what you get:

Figure 3.1, Screenshot of the Keywords Everywhere plug-in in action

Below the search box you'll see: Volume: 1,300/mo. This means that 1,300 people a month are typing "moving to Nashville" into the Google search bar.

CPC: $7.57. This means the cost per click is $7.57. If you were to run a Google pay-per-click ad, you could expect to pay $7.57 per click—yikes! That's pretty pricey, but it means that it's a keyword that performs well for advertisers, so they're willing to pay that. For our purposes, we won't pay any attention to this number other than to say, "Hahaha, suckers! I'm getting this traffic for free, and you're probably paying $1000/month for it!"

Competition: 0.3. This is how competitive that keyword is to rank for organically. Organic = free. This number is on a scale of 0.01 to 1.00. The lower the number the easier it will be to rank for. So 0.3 means there is almost NO competition.

I consider anything from 0 – .33 low, .34 – .66 medium, and .67+ high. When we do keyword research, we're looking for something with low competition.

In this example, Moving to Nashville is a killer keyword! It gets plenty of search traffic and the competition is low, which means it should be easy to rank for.

Now, keep in mind that this tool, Keywords Everywhere, is evaluating the internet as a whole, not only the searches done on YouTube. But Google owns YouTube, so your videos can also show up on the first page of Google.

There also seem to be far more articles on any given topic than videos about 99% of the time. So, if it is a good keyword on Google, it's probably going to be an amazing keyword for YouTube.

When you type in your keyword idea, you will also see a bar down the side of the screen with two boxes that say Related Keywords and People Also Search For.

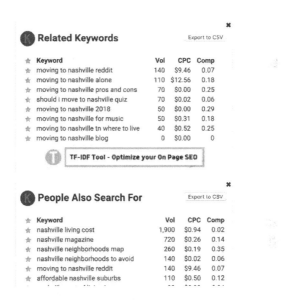

Related Keywords			Export to CSV
Keyword	Vol	CPC	Comp
moving to nashville reddit	140	$9.46	0.07
moving to nashville alone	110	$12.56	0.18
moving to nashville pros and cons	70	$0.00	0.25
should i move to nashville quiz	70	$0.02	0.06
moving to nashville 2018	50	$0.00	0.29
moving to nashville for music	50	$0.31	0.18
moving to nashville tn where to live	40	$0.52	0.25
moving to nashville blog	0	$0.00	0

TF-IDF Tool - Optimize your On Page SEO

People Also Search For			Export to CSV
Keyword	Vol	CPC	Comp
nashville living cost	1,900	$0.94	0.02
nashville magazine	720	$0.26	0.14
nashville neighborhoods map	260	$0.19	0.35
nashville neighborhoods to avoid	140	$0.02	0.06
moving to nashville reddit	140	$9.46	0.07
affordable nashville suburbs	110	$0.50	0.12

Figure 3.2, Screenshot of the Keywords Everywhere sidebar

If your original search shows you that there is very little search volume for that keyword, or if it has a really high competition score, check out the sidebar for some other ideas.

For example, you could try the keyword Nashville living cost. It gets 1,900 searches with almost no competition. That would make a great video topic!

In fact, this is such a great keyword that your video could be *mediocre at best* and still rank #1. It doesn't need to win an Academy Award; it only needs to be interesting to watch and full of good information.

Another good tool for planning your videos is TubeBuddy - https://www.tubebuddy.com/KarinCarr(*).

TubeBuddy has a free version, and they have paid versions of various levels, but the free version is pretty sweet. I used the free version for quite a while before I went to the Pro version because they were having a killer sale. Just visit the Tubebuddy site for the differences between the paid and free versions.

Now, I'm going to go on record and say that I *do not use* TubeBuddy for keyword research. We REALTORS® are hyperlocal business owners. I can't sell a house in Maryland or Michigan. I sell only in Georgia, and specifically in the Savannah area.

> *In my humble opinion, a keyword that gets only 75 searches a month but indicates that they are looking to make a buying decision in my area can be a very profitable keyword!*

"Moving to Savannah" gets less than 100 searches a month, but that keyword has easily made me $100,000 in the last two years alone. Yet TubeBuddy says that "Moving to Savannah" is a poor keyword because the search volume is low and there's quite a bit of competition.

TubeBuddy feels that something that gets so little search volume a month isn't worth going after. I disagree wholeheartedly. Moving to Savannah shows high intent on the part of the person doing the search. They would not be Googling moving to Savannah if they were not going to be moving to Savannah! And if they move, they're going to need a place to live. Not all of them want to buy, of course, but a lot of them do. And even renters can eventually become buyers.

TubeBuddy also says there's a lot of competition for that keyword. Most of them are vlogs, not videos done by real estate agents. There are tons of travel videos and just people saying, "Hey, I'm moving! Follow my journey." So, no, there's not much competition.

You might be wondering why I even bother with TubeBuddy if I'm not using it to find keywords.

My absolute favorite reason for using TubeBuddy is that it lets you analyze your competition's videos, see what tags they are using, and how they are ranking. It also shows you how well your own videos are performing.

You can analyze what other YouTubers are doing and then improve upon it with your own videos. TubeBuddy also lets you make custom thumbnails and do a bunch of other things, and many of these are even available with the free version. So, I recommend you get it but don't worry if it says your keyword stinks. Stick with Keywords Everywhere for keyword research.

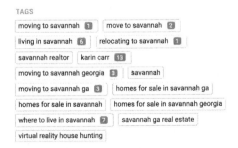

Figure 3.3, Screenshot of how the tags for my Moving to Savannah video are ranking according to TubeBuddy

Between Keywords Everywhere and TubeBuddy (or any other keyword research tool you care to use), you will get great ideas for topics people are actually searching for. And this is the key!

> *You have to make videos with keywords people are searching for if you want to get views, calls, and clients!*

Here are some typical video titles I see on YouTube.

> *Pete's vlog episode #37*
> *One Minute Wednesday - Let's talk mortgages*
> *Joe Brown, REALTOR® - Marvelous home on the ocean*
> *Another happy seller in West Bloomfield*
> *New listing by XYZ Brokerage in South Jordan*

Would you ever type any of these things into the search bar? Nope. Neither does anyone else. That's why they all only get 12 views.

YouTube is a search engine, not a social media platform. Once you understand this concept, your video titles will be 100x better and have a much better chance of ranking on page one.

I met an agent from Vancouver at a conference recently. We had a great conversation about this topic of keyword research. He is fantastic on camera and was putting out a lot of video on Facebook but hadn't really considered using YouTube. I then proceeded to nag him for the next half hour about using YouTube until he finally caved in.

A few weeks after the conference, he texted me and said:

"The first of my educational videos on YouTube dropped today."

The next morning, he said:

"Update! After only 24 hours, this video is already ranking #2 in Google search results! I can't believe it."

Did you catch that? *He said he's ranking on Google, not on YouTube!* The sweet spot for the ideal search volume seems to be less than 1,000 searches a month (while your channel is still small - 100 subscribers or less) but more than 70 if at all possible. Otherwise there's just not enough interest in that topic.

Remember that these keywords should have low to medium-low competition. The lower, the better. A keyword that has a competition score of .86 is much harder to rank for than one that has a competition score of .13.

If it gets 50,000 searches a month, you will also probably have a really hard time ranking for that because your channel is new and doesn't have enough traffic yet, not enough authority in the eyes of YouTube. You can go after the more competitive keywords later when your channel takes off.

Even if a keyword has only 100 searches a month, that's still 100 potential clients who didn't know your name a month ago.

And now, they do.

◆ ◆ ◆

YOUTUBER ACTION ITEM #3

Your assignment today is to do keyword research for your video topic ideas.

Think of your ideal customer avatar. Remember when we determined who they are and what their challenges are? Make a list of five to ten things they probably have questions about.

Install Keywords Everywhere and do some keyword research. Keep in mind you may have to try ten variations of the keyword until you find one that has 70 - 1,000 monthly searches and has a low competition score. It's ok— look at what Keywords Everywhere says people are also searching for down the right side of your computer screen.

Here's an example. I did this exercise with one of my students in Canada this morning. She picked new construction as her niche. Her idea for a video topic was "Why use a Realtor to buy a new build" but that keyword gets zero searches each month.

However, Keywords Everywhere suggested "new construction home buying process" and that is a perfect keyword! Almost 500 searches a month and medium-low competition.

It's ok if you have to tweak your keyword until you find just the right phrase. Write down the keyword word for word, the monthly search volume, and the competition score.

For example, I have an idea to do a video comparing Atlanta to Savannah—which is better? Here is my list of keyword research results:

> *Atlanta or Savannah - 20 searches a month, .00 competition*
> *Atlanta vs Savannah - 40 searches, .00 competition*
> *Savannah vs Atlanta - 110 searches, .03 competition*

By keeping track of keywords that are potential titles, the big winners will clearly stand out. Savannah vs Atlanta wins hands down. It has much more search volume and still has next to no competition. (Remember, a competition score of less than .33 is what we are looking for whenever possible.)

Pick four to five keywords that will be good video topics for your ideal customer and your niche. If your niche is urban professionals living in condos who don't want to mow grass because they work all day, brainstorm topics they would find interesting. What do HOA fees cover, best high end condos in your city, are condos pet friendly, where to live if you work at XXX major employer, etc. These will be the first four videos you create.

Congratulations! You've just come up with a month's worth of video topics.

DAY FOUR: CHANNEL ART

In today's challenge, we are going to overhaul your YouTube cover photo—also known as channel art. You channel art is extremely important.

A good cover photo should do the following:

1. *Show your face*
2. *Tell everyone where you are geographically located*
3. *Have whatever brokerage information is legally required in your area*
4. *Tell people what they will learn on your channel—in other words, give them a reason to subscribe*
5. *Declare to the world your upload schedule*

Let's dive into each of these a little deeper. You want to show your face because you are your brand. We want people to arrive at your channel and immediately put a face to the name. *Yes, you need to be smiling.*

Next, you want to tell them where you're located, because if you live in Orlando and the viewer is in Saskatchewan, they need to know right away whether you're in their market or in the market they want to move to.

You probably also need to disclose that you're a real estate licensee and who your broker is. Tell them whatever is legally required by your state. If you're not certain, just Google whatever your area's real estate governing board is called. Mine is GREC (the Georgia Real Estate Commission) but if you are not sure what yours is, just ask your broker. They most likely have a section for licensees on their web site that lists out their advertising policies.

Next, you need to tell viewers what's in it for them. Why should they subscribe? What will they learn on your channel? This can be something simple like "Provo, UT, neighborhood tours" or "Helping our veterans find homes in Sarasota, FL."

Finally, tell them how often you will be uploading. This serves two purposes:

> *1. If they know how often to expect new videos, they are more likely to subscribe, and they will eagerly await new content.*
> *2. There is no better accountability partner than declaring to the entire world you will post new videos every Thursday.*

I am very proud to say I've only missed one day in two years, and that was when we had to evacuate for Hurricane Irma. So, I had a good reason, but had I planned better, it wouldn't have put me behind schedule.

Once or twice, I've posted much later in the day than I usually do, and it really ticked me off that people noticed! I usually publish at 9 a.m., and someone mentioned on Facebook at lunchtime one day that I hadn't posted yet. He called me out in public—so rude!

I was annoyed at the time because I was already stressing big time, trying to get this damned video up at all. But once I hit publish, I calmed down and realized people were anxiously awaiting my content. The fact that they noticed I hadn't published a video yet showed me that people were actually watching my videos and liked them enough to notice when one was late. How flattering is that?

When you are creating your channel art, it doesn't have to be elaborate with tons of graphics. It needs to be easy to read, not terribly busy, and it should fit your brand. Remember that more than 50% of the people are watching on their phones. So, your channel art must be legible on a tiny screen.

The challenge is to make something that looks great and has all the info necessary without looking too busy ... and it should fit on a screen that's only a few inches across.

◆ ◆ ◆

YOUTUBER ACTION ITEM #4

Your assignment is to make your channel art. You can use Picmonkey, Canva, Photoshop, or any graphic design app that you like to use.

I like Canva.com, and I use it almost daily. You can use it to make social media images, flyers, posters, presentations, trim-fold brochures, lead magnets (which we'll talk about tomorrow), custom thumbnail images, and channel art.

Go to Canva.com and choose the YouTube channel art template but let me caution you—the only part of the design that will show up on a mobile device is whatever is in the very center of the design. The dimensions of the template assume you're watching a YouTube video on your smart TV, which has miles of real estate compared to a phone.

Figure 4.1, Screenshot of the YouTube channel art dimensions template

So, to make your life easier, download this template from You-Tube with the exact dimensions required, and then upload it into Canva. https://support.google.com/youtube/answer/2972003

Or you can download my free template which is already sized for you with the four required elements right there front and center. All you have to do is change the colors and text, add your photo and logo, and it's ready to upload. You can get it here: https://www.YouTubesuccesschecklist.com/free-channel-art-template/

You could even hire someone on Fiverr (*) to make it for you but make sure it includes the elements listed above.

Don't spend more than an hour on this if you make it yourself. You can go down the rabbit hole and spend hours and hours messing with your channel art design, trust me. Been there, done that. Remember that you can change it anytime you want.

Just make one now, and if you want to change the colors or the font later, it's totally fine. The point is to get it done as soon as you can, and upload that baby to your channel!

DAY FIVE: A GOOD CALL-TO-ACTION (CTA)

Today, we're going to discuss how to wrap up your video at the end, and what to say to get someone to take action. This is called a call-to-action, or CTA.

Your CTA cannot be, "If you are thinking of buying or selling in the Detroit metro area, call me! I'd love to assist you. You can reach me at 313-555-1212. " You've probably said that plenty of times before in videos, haven't you? Mmm hmmm. How has that worked out for you so far? Is your phone ringing off the hook?

You probably got seven likes and six were from other agents, one was from a former client, and the comments section is like a ghost town. I used to do it all the time myself. Believe me, I'm not judging.

But if we now know that it doesn't work, how about trying something that does?

You need to be helpful and offer something valuable to the viewer —and ask for nothing in return. I know, I know, it sounds counter-intuitive. It goes against everything our trainers and coaches have taught us. We've got to do trial closes, we've got to ask for the sale—not once but three times!

I'm telling you, YouTube is different. People don't go to YouTube looking to buy something; they go to learn something.

> *You should offer them something they would find valuable, something they would be willing to trade their contact information for in order to get.*

So, what can you offer them without making it sound like a giant sales pitch? It should be relevant to the video.

For example, I recently recorded a video called "Retiring in Savannah, GA." I know my niche (people relocating to Savannah), and I did my keyword research (it gets 260 searches a month and has low competition), so I offered a free relocation guide at the end of the video.

Here are my results. 69 views and 38 downloads in three months.

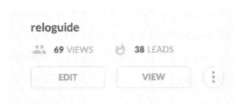

Figure 5.1, Screenshot from my web site analytics of the number of people who have visited my relocation guide landing page

My team has followed up with all 38 leads and we have converted a ton of them into clients already. Some aren't retiring here for several years but many are ready to move in the next few months. And when we call them they are excited to talk to us!

With some good videos and good lead magnets you can easily grow your database of prospective clients. I have over 1000 people in my LionDesk database by using this method.

But I know what you're thinking. *How the heck can I create a whole relocation guide? Who's got time for that?* Well, let me ask you this ... would you spend a few hours to make one if you knew it would make you $10,000 in return? Or better yet, would you hire a Virtual Assistant for $100 to make it for you if you knew it would bring you tons of business? Yeah, I would too!

Here's how I made mine. I went to my city's chamber of commerce web site and downloaded their relocation guide. It's about 80 pages long, and 70 pages are advertisements for my competitors.

So, I looked at the ten pages of real info, and while it was ok, it was still pretty generic. I figured I could make one that was way better, so I took their idea and 10X'ed it. (Is that a word? Well, it is now.)

I used Canva to make it, using one of their brochure templates. I added my name and logo, my contact info on the last page, and changed the colors to match my brand.

Here is a sample page:

Figure 5.2, One of the pages in my relocation guide

That hyperlink is a link to one of my YouTube videos. It's a clickable link because they download this guide as a PDF. In that video, I talk about the different areas around Savannah. When they watch it, I get even more face time with them, so they get to know me better, which cements our relationship that much more. Score!

I have tons of helpful information that's all about Savannah, not all about me and how fabulous I am. Other than my logo at the bottom of each page (and I really did that only so people can't steal it and pass it off as their own), there's very little information about me.

Finally, on the last page, I added my contact info, how they can reach me, and special services I offer to buyers who are relocating. Yes, another CTA!

So, back to the call to action in the video itself. At the end of the video I said,

> *"If you are thinking of retiring to Savannah, I have a free relocation guide that you are welcome to download. Just click the link below to get a copy right now."*

That's it. No sales pitch, no flashing your phone number on the screen. No begging for their business! No one likes the smell of desperation, so don't act desperate. You've got this free thing. If they want it, cool. And if they don't, that's ok too.

Now, of course you are going to put it on a landing page (don't worry, I'll explain landing pages in a few minutes) so that they are prompted to enter their name, email address, and phone number to get it. And nine times out of ten, you'll get real contact info because they are probably thinking of retiring in Savannah if they Googled retiring in Savannah. And if they want the relocation guide and they like you, they put in real information. Not every time but most of the time.

> *By NOT asking for the business, you get more business. It's a head scratcher, but I've been testing this for two years. It works, y'all.*

Now for the techie stuff.

You will need a few things to do this well:

> *A web page where people will fill out the form*
> *A way to deliver the freebie they are requesting*
> *A way to follow up with them automatically*

Let's tackle each one of these things in more detail. You'll need to have a web site with landing pages OR have a standalone landing page software solution.

> *A landing page is just a single page where the visitor either*

fills out a form to get what you're offering, or they leave. There are no navigation buttons so they can't go read your blog or start searching for homes. A landing page encourages a visitor to do one thing and one thing only - give you their contact information.

I use Easy Agent Pro(*) as my web site provider. I have been a client of theirs for several years, and I love them because I can make unlimited landing pages. But if you just want a landing page software solution instead of a full web site try Leadpages(*). This is what I use for advertising my coaching program, YouTube for Agents.

If you have a very basic web site that your brokerage gives you without any landing pages, you'll have to pony up some cash. Sorry.

Even if you have a site provide by your brokerage that can display all the listings in your MLS, and also allows for blogging and maybe even some landing pages, what happens if you switch brokerages? You lose all that information because it's not your own web site.

The same goes for using your brokerage-given email address for creating your YouTube channel. Don't do it! I've seen people lose their entire channel when they switched brokerages. Do yourself a favor and create a Gmail email address just for your channel.

You can try a site like MailChimp, which will give you landing pages for free, but they recently revamped their pricing structure. You'll have to do some research to see if you can make landing pages with their free plan. You'll want to invest in a good tool that will automatically reply to their request with a nice little thank you message and the freebie attached. Bonus points if it will automatically start sending them emails and/or text messages that are customized based on what freebie they downloaded.

For example, if they download the relo guide you want to assume they're thinking of moving to your area. So have an email drip and/or text message drip campaign that starts automatically that asks about their plans for relocating.

I use LionDesk (*) as my customer relationship management (CRM) system because it does all those things. It's pretty inexpensive for a CRM that's specifically made for REALTORS®. I've met the owner before (ok, one time for about five minutes at a real estate conference and I didn't know he was the owner for the first three minutes we were talking), and he told me the story of why he created this program. He seemed like a really nice guy, and I've been extremely happy with LionDesk in the years I've used them. It is not the easiest interface to learn, but it has a ton of features, so if you can get over the initial hurdle of learning to use it, there are a million cool things it can do.

Back to the freebies. *You don't need a different freebie or lead magnet for every video.* You only need a handful that you can use over and over again. A few for sellers, a few for buyers, maybe a few for specific loan types, or for specific neighborhoods.

You will spend the time up front to create them once in order to use them 20 times. Once again, they're going to fill in real contact info most of the time because they know, like, and trust you by now. And when I call them and say, "Hi, Joe! This is Karin Carr. I saw that you just downloaded my relocation guide. Are you thinking of moving to Savannah?" They typically say something along the lines of:

"Oh, my gosh, I can't believe you called me! You're a celebrity! You must be so busy. Thank you for calling me! Yes, we are moving and want to buy a house when we get there. I loved your video about Tybee Island, but you said they're prone to hurricanes. But then in the video about Pooler, you said that almost none of those houses require flood insurance, so we're a little torn. We'd love you to represent us, though! My husband was just offered a job with XXX major employer, and I'm a teacher, so I'll have to find a job once I get there. And we have two kids— they're seven and ten—so good schools are really important. I'm so glad we found you; your videos have been so helpful!"

I'm not exaggerating. This right here is why I haven't missed uploading a video in two years (except during Irma—thanks a lot, Irma).

What if you're trying to attract sellers? If your video was all about staging on a budget, at the end, you could say, "So, now you know how to make your house look great if you're getting ready to sell. But do you know what you need to do to get it sold fast? No worries, I've got a free report for you called 'Five Tips to Selling Your Home in Thirty Days.'"

Think of your niche, who you want to attract, and something valuable you could offer them as a freebie. Make it relevant to the video topic. I think it goes without saying that you wouldn't offer a staging guide to a first-time buyer.

Don't worry about how pretty it looks. It can be a Word document you saved as a PDF. Canva will make it pretty if you want to spend some time (or have a virtual assistant do it) but it can seriously be a black and white text document. If it has good information in it, that's all that matters.

I made one lead magnet that was a Home Inspection Checklist. It's a Microsoft Word doc of things the home inspector is looking for during a home inspection. I found all the information on the internet and compiled the list in Word. Then I changed up the wording so I wasn't plagiarizing.

As of the time of this publication, it's had eighty-six views, and I've gotten twenty-seven leads. The people see the video on You-Tube, and if they want the freebie, they can click the link in the description box below.

If your channel supports cards, you can have a clickable link in your video, but YouTube changed the requirements in 2018 for people to be able to use cards in their videos. If you have fewer than 1,000 subscribers and 4,000 hours of watch time, your channel is probably not eligible yet, so put the link in the description box below the video. You can even say, "Click the link below" and point down to show them where exactly that URL is to download your free checklist.

> *Not everybody will fill out the form. That's fine. We are weeding out the tire kickers.*

I don't want to waste my time following up with you if you're not planning to buy or sell a house in my market anytime in the next few years, or if you just don't want to talk to me. I don't have time to call 86 people if only 17 are even remotely interested.

You know how they say lead gen is a numbers game, and you have to follow up with everyone an average of 7-12 times before you get anywhere?

I call bullshit on that.

If they were serious about buying or selling and knew who you were and they were actually considering hiring you, your conversation rate would go from 3% to about 70% overnight. You'd get fewer leads, but the ones you got would be a million times better. I'd rather have 5 solid leads than 100 that kind of suck, wouldn't you?

Here's a question I get asked a lot. Should you use a lead magnet at the end of every single video? My answer is... no.

> *Most of the time you want to keep people on YouTube because you will get rewarded by the algorithm if you can bring people to their platform and keep them there. If you always drive people away from the platform, you'll be penalized. As in your videos won't show up in search as much. And if they don't show up in search results, no one can watch them.*

So, I usually have a CTA asking them to watch another video. "If you liked this video, you should check out the one I did about XYZ" and link to that video. In the beginning, you can't do this because you don't have any other videos to link to. But once you have uploaded five to ten videos, you can start mentioning them as you are recording. Tell people to click the link to watch another video and often they will do it!

Here's a good rule of thumb. Do that for three videos in a row, and then on the fourth one, direct them to your website and give them something for free. Not only can you capture their information if they fill out the form, but you can also retarget them on

Facebook later if you have installed the Facebook pixel on your web site, even if they didn't fill out the form. But that's a whole other subject for a whole different book.

YOUTUBER ACTION ITEM #5

Think of the video topics you came up with on Day Three. What would a good lead magnet be for two of those videos? Jot down some ideas here. Now open up Word, Pages, or whatever program you use and see if you can bang out a one- to two-page-document. Don't worry about formatting— do a brain dump into this document. You can make it pretty later. Right now, we only want the basic outline.

Again, you can have a virtual assistant or someone on Fiverr format it for you once you have gathered all the info that needs to be in it. Make sure it's helpful, doesn't come across as a giant sales pitch, and include all your contact info either on the first or the last page.

Once it's done, save it as a PDF, slap your contact info and logo on the last page, and you're good to go.

Now that that's done, let's conquer the biggest obstacle of all... YOU.

DAY SIX: CONQUER YOUR FEAR

Welcome to Day Six! Today is going to be a pretty intense topic. It's a heavy concept, but it's also life transforming.

We're going to talk about mindset and how to conquer your fear of being on camera. I talk to agents every day who say they would make more videos … if only they could lose twenty pounds first. Or if they were younger.

They say they can't make videos because they don't know what to do, they don't have the time, they don't want their wrinkles to be on display, or they aren't interesting enough.

You've all heard the saying, "Whether you think you can or you can't, you're right." This is 100% true when it comes to being successful on YouTube.

If you are telling yourself, "This will take too much time. Editing my videos will be too hard. I don't have the right equipment. I'm too fat to be on camera. No one cares what I have to say. Other agents are so much more successful than I am! Why would anyone care about my videos? I've only been licensed a year. I don't have enough experience. I'm not good enough. I'm not interesting enough."

You, my friend, are absolutely right.

Because if that's what you believe, of course you're right. A belief is simply a thought that you repeat over and over to yourself until you believe it. Once you believe it, that becomes your reality. You are convinced it's true, so you act as though it's true, and as a result, your actions make it true.

> *Your subconscious mind wants you to always be right, so you will subconsciously do things that prove that by God, you're right!*

If you tell yourself this won't work because there's too much competition in your market, your subconscious mind will do whatever it has to do to prove you right. By telling yourself you can't do it over and over and over again, you start to believe it. Once you believe it, you act as if it's true, and therefore, you make it true.

Knock that shit off!

When I started making weekly videos, I knew without a shadow of a doubt it would work to get me business because it *already had gotten me business*. That man had called me right after I moved to Savannah, and he and his wife wanted to work with me because they'd been watching my videos. Because I already knew it would work, I never once doubted myself. I believed it would work so I acted as though it worked, and lo and behold, it worked!

If you tell yourself that this strategy will work and that you are good at this over and over again, eventually, you start to believe it. Once you believe it, you act as though it's true, so it becomes true.

It truly is that simple.

You need to act as though it's already working. Act as though you are already getting new clients who say they found you on You-Tube. They are so grateful to have found your videos. You have answered their questions and made the buying or selling process much less scary. They appreciate you and they respect your advice. Act as though you have valuable information to share—because you do!

> *Believe that you are providing information to people who desperately need your services and expertise. Your #1 goal in making these videos is to let them get to know you and to provide as much value to the viewer—and here's the kicker—while expecting nothing in return.*

When you give with no expectation of getting anything back, that's when you get something back. It's ironic, don'tcha think? That's the whole premise behind content marketing. Gary Vaynerchuk wrote a whole book about this called *Jab Jab Jab Right Hook*. Give, give, give, and then ask the viewer to do something.

So, don't think about all the reasons why this YouTube video strategy thing won't work. I give you permission NOT to think about what could go wrong.

I give you permission to think that everything is going to work out in your favor. That marketing your business on YouTube is going to be amazing for your business, life, happiness, well-being, and mental state. That you will become a little mini celebrity in your market.

I give you permission to have fun making videos, to cut yourself some slack at the beginning when you look like a deer in the headlights. To forgive yourself for tripping over your words and making mistakes and having to film your video four times before you finally get it right.

I give you permission.

Beginning today, before you press the record button, remember that it's all about the viewer. It's not about you; it's about providing value to your audience. You are helping them with one of the biggest financial transactions they're probably ever going to make. You are there to alleviate their concerns, educate them, guide them, make the process easier, and help build their wealth. They need you, and dammit, they are lucky to have you!

Here are five tips to help you get out of your own head:

1: Nobody cares what you look like. Do you refuse to meet clients now because you need to lose ten pounds? Of course not. It's not about what you look like. It's about saving them thousands of dollars; finding their dream home; or selling a home they acquired because their father died, and they were going through one of the most stressful periods of their lives.

These people must make big decisions, and they need help from an expert. You are that expert. Does it really matter what color your hair is? By refusing to get on camera you are refusing to help these people. You are thinking only about yourself, and that's just plain selfish. But you are not selfish, you are doing this to help others. So, think about them, and forget about what you look like.

2: Remember you are attracting your ideal client, your tribe if you will. Remember how we picked our niche on day one? You're attracting your tribe by the nature of your videos. Not only by the subject matter but also by the personality you display on camera.

If someone doesn't like your personality, they won't call you. So what? They didn't call, but you don't know that they didn't call, so there's no rejection. You have so much value to offer, and if they can't see that, you don't want them as a client anyway.

3: You will get better from the sheer repetition of making videos over and over again. Remember when you had first gotten your license? I bet the first time you showed properties you were pretty nervous. You wanted to sound like you knew what you were doing, and you were praying they didn't ask you how long you'd been in real estate. I didn't even know how to open the lockbox, and I was terrified I'd look stupid in front of my clients.

Do you get nervous now when you show a house? No. Why not? Because you've done it over and over again. Competence = confidence. When you get competent with this process of making videos, you will naturally feel more confident about it, and your confidence comes through on camera. The sheer repetition will make you more confident in your ability. And that really does come across on camera.

4: 80% of your communication is nonverbal. I'm talking body language, your tone of voice, and eye contact. Only 20% is from the actual words you say. So, don't stress if you stumble over your words, or you say the wrong word by accident. Your smile, tone, and generosity of spirit will be what make people listen to you. You can always fix a mistake in post-production when you're doing a little bit of editing.

5: But the best way to get over your fear of being on camera is to make a conscious decision not to give a flying #@$! what other people think. The beauty of getting older is that you don't care what people think anymore.

I turned 50 this year, and this has been one of the best years of my entire career. I'm good at what I do. I have helped hundreds of real estate agents turn their businesses around and become profitable for the first time ever. I have a team of agents in Savannah that get motivated leads handed to them on a silver platter every day, and all they have to do is go sell them a house. I feel pretty damned good about that!

Being young and skinny is not a requirement to be successful. Neither is having sold 100 homes. If somebody doesn't call you because they didn't connect with you on video, that's perfectly fine. You don't like everyone you meet, and they don't all have to like you.

> But I'll tell you one thing they're not going to do. They're not going to call you and say, "Hi, Jenny. You know, I almost hired you to sell my house. But you're thirty pounds over-weight, so I reconsidered." That will never, ever happen.

They also will not call to say, "I was this close to hiring you, but I found your editing skills to be lacking. I don't like your graphics or your font choice."

Will there be trolls on the Internet that are going to say nasty things in the comments? Probably. I've had some doozies myself!

When you put yourself out there and you're making yourself vulnerable, you open yourself up to that possibility. They will make snide comments below the video because it's totally anonymous for them. They will say things they would never have the guts to say to your face.

> *The beauty of YouTube is that it's your channel. You control the content on your channel. If somebody writes a nasty comment, you can delete them, and you can block them from ever commenting on your channel again. Problem solved.*

The first time I got a thumbs down on a video I was like, "Waaaaah, why don't they like me? I can't believe that they didn't like my video!" I cracked open a bottle of wine that night and whined to my husband, who totally didn't understand why a complete stranger whose face I'd never seen and whose name I didn't know hurt my feelings.

The next day, I told myself it wasn't me he didn't like; it was Savannah. It gets hot and humid here, so he doesn't want to live here. Ok, I can live with that. And I then promptly forgot about him and have made 200 videos since then.

Another time I was doing a live webinar. I was giving my back-story so the agents watching would know how I arrived at this strategy and why I knew it would work. After all, any Internet marketing guru can tell you to do XYZ and you'll make a million dollars. I wanted to show that I'd been in their shoes, and I understood their struggles.

This one guy said all I did was brag about myself. Ouch, that stung. That one really hurt my feelings. I coach agents because I truly want to help them improve their careers and make more money while actually improving their quality of life. The course I created was a labor of love, and the fact that I can earn a living doing this now is a bonus.

So, I thought about what he said. I did some real soul searching ... for about five whole minutes. And then I decided it was utter bullshit. He doesn't know me, he doesn't know my motivation, and he doesn't know what's in my heart. He was probably having a bad day and was projecting onto me, so I rejected his opinion and never gave it another thought.

They say when you start getting haters, you know you've made it. You're making enough of an impact in your community that people are seeing what you're doing.

> *If you don't have haters, it's probably because nobody knows you exist.*

Are you willing to have one or two haters if you're closing 20 extra deals a year? I watched a non-real estate video yesterday that had 70,000 views. She had 350 likes and 64 dislikes. Do you think the 64 dislikes are keeping her up at night when she's getting 70,000 views on each of her videos? I highly doubt it.

When you get your first nasty comment, it's almost like a badge of honor. It's a rite of passage. And if some people have such low opinions of themselves that the way they feel better is by making snarky comments on your channel, then I feel sad for them.

> *When someone makes a snarky comment on your video, it speaks more to their character than yours.*

You cannot let your insecurities, whether it's about your ability, your experience, or your appearance, stop you! Because everyone else is letting it stop them.

There's a reason why all the fellow agents in your market are not doing this. It's because they are too self-conscious for video marketing. And the only way to really fail is to not even try at all.

So, get over your damned self! You'll be the one out there doing it and dominating your market in no time.

YOUTUBER ACTION ITEM #6

Think about some of the YouTube channels you like to watch. Why do you like to watch them? Is it because of how they look, or is it because of how they make you feel? (Don't include beauty tutorials, because come on, they're all gorgeous and will make us feel like crap about ourselves.)

Do you laugh watching them? Do they make you feel empowered? If it's a DIY tutorial, does it make you feel like you could actually do this? Do they inspire you to do something or be something? After you watch these videos, are you encouraged or uplifted? Or do they just explain concepts in a way that you understand so you walk away feeling like you actually learned something?

Make a list of all the qualities you have that make you the perfect person to solve a potential client's problems. Because that's really all that the viewers want. They want a real person that they trust to help them, and they want to like that person. They won't hire a REALTOR® to sell their house no matter how competent that person is if they don't like him or her.

If you want to really get into the positive affirmation stuff, check out this recording by Bob Baker. I love this guy!

You are supposed to listen to this short affirmation every morning for twenty-one days in a row. I wake up early, grab a cup of coffee, and sit out on my screened porch and listen to this before my family gets up.

I dare you not to feel like a rock star after telling yourself this for three solid weeks. https://youtu.be/v5PKj2k3DY4

DAY SEVEN: TIME MANAGEMENT

Congratulations! You made it to the last day of this challenge!

I got a little heavy on you yesterday, I know. But I've now coached hundreds of agents (and a few loan officers) across the world, and I'm finding there is only one thing that separates the ones who are finding success on YouTube and the ones who aren't.

It's not your market or how much competition there is, and it's definitely not what you look like. Pretty sure you can guess by now what that is. It's your attitude, your confidence on camera, and unwavering belief that this will work as a lead generation strategy for your business.

The more presentations I give on using YouTube the more I find myself talking about mindset. Everyone wants to know about the equipment I use, the editing software, and whether I use a teleprompter. They want to know what I use for editing. They get caught up in the stuff, the one thing I must be doing or a piece of equipment or software I have that is getting me tons of business. The honest truth is that those things are the least important part of this process. Because the thing that determines their success is the story they tell themselves.

Tell yourself you're fan-freaking-tastic and believe it. The end.

The final topic for this challenge is finding the time to actually do this—and to be consistent. We all have the same 24 hours in a day. How you choose to spend those hours is up to you.

I mentioned before that the word grind is not in my vocabulary. I don't think you need to get five hours of sleep each night so you can squeeze in time to make a video.

Now if you are starting this journey with NO VIDEO EX-PERIENCE AT ALL, it's going to take more time. It might take you two hours to film your first few videos because you make so many mistakes. That's ok! I promise you will get better.

And when you edit your first video it's going to seem like it takes you All. Freaking. Day. If you have never used video editing software before, it very well might. Because first you have to learn how to use it, and then you have to learn how to make your video look more interesting.

I had a student say the other day that she literally spent all day working on her first video. She was frustrated and wondered how on earth she would ever be able to keep this up long-term.

My answer was, the first time you went bowling did you get 10 strikes? The first time you went skiing did you ski the black diamond runs? No, of course not. No one expects you to be a pro right from the beginning.

Editing is a skill that you have to learn, but the more you do it the better and faster you get. I used to spend about four to six hours a week editing each video I made. That was just editing, not including filming and uploading! Then I got more familiar with the editing software and learned a few secrets to shorten up that process and got it down to more like three to four hours a week.

Now I have a VA who does all my editing so I spend more like 90 minutes a week between keyword research, filming, and writing the description that goes below the video on YouTube. But when I was doing it all myself that was about half an hour a day.

Can you find half an hour to an hour a day? If not, could you skip doing something that's less important? Watching TV? Surfing social media mindlessly? I'd gladly trade door knocking for video production.

Now don't jump down my throat and insist that door knocking works. I'm sure that it does ... sometimes.

But I'd rather spend a few hours making a video that will bring me business for years to come than door knock when it's 95 degrees outside and 1000% humidity, hoping that five people will actually answer their door.

With door knocking when I get in my car and drive away, that's it. There's no more lead generation going on. I'm done. Compare that to a good YouTube video. If you use the right keyword, it has the potential to bring you thousands of views, and when you're getting thousands of views, you get plenty of clients.

YouTube brings my entire team a consistent stream of leads week in and week out. My Moving to Savannah video has over 15,000 views right now and it brings us leads almost daily.

Have I convinced you yet? Good.

First, pick a day of the week to record. I randomly chose Thursdays because we don't seem to ever have office meetings on Thursdays. I figured I'd send the kids off to school, get showered, put on some makeup, and record at 9:30 am. You can do whatever day and time works for you, but I like having the house to myself. It's totally quiet and no one is listening to me mess up over and over again.

Then, I did something crazy. Something totally outrageous—I put it on my calendar. Yep, I scheduled it as a weekly recurring appointment with no end date. And if someone says, "Can you show me five houses on Thursday morning? I'm preapproved for a million dollars," I tell them, "I'm afraid I already have a commitment Thursday morning, but how about if we meet at noon instead?"

Filming your video is an appointment. It is an appointment that has the potential to bring you a crapload of business, clients, and commission checks. *Do not cancel.*

If you absolutely must cancel (your grandfather's funeral is an acceptable excuse), you have to reschedule it and film the day before or the day after. But this will not be a regular occurrence. Got it?

Because here's the thing... I hear people say all the time that they took the summer off, or the kids got sick so they skipped a week, or they went on vacation and didn't post a video that week so they're playing catch up.

Commitment is not just about keeping your word to other people. It's about keeping your word... period.

Now you will pick the day you plan to upload. Again, you can pick whatever day/time you want. Don't agonize over when you think you will get the most views. Once you have a bunch of videos uploaded and a lot of views, you can review your analytics and see when most people are watching. But I really don't think it matters.

My most popular videos were made at least a year ago. Did all those people watch it the day the videos came out? No. They watched it when they searched for the keyword, whenever that might have been. In fact, I think I probably picked the worst day and time to publish based on when people are online watching videos—Monday morning at 9 a.m. People are just getting to work (or still sleeping if they're on the west coast) and catching up from the weekend. They're probably working and not screwing around watching YouTube videos. But consistency is the key. I picked a day and time, and I stuck with it. I could change it but, hey, if it ain't broke ...

Once you get the hang of filming, you can bang out a video in half an hour or less. In fact, I recorded a real time video recently where I did my keyword research (took about ten minutes) and filmed the video (took eleven minutes). If you want to check it out, you can watch it here: How to Plan and Record a Video - Real Time - https://youtu.be/Z-qY2EtAylU

Next you'll want to start batch filming. This one thing will be a lifesaver many times over.

Batch filming is where you set up the camera, lights, and microphone, and you get yourself camera-ready, but you record several videos back to back.

If you can spend two hours and record a month's worth of videos, that is time well spent. Since you already did your keyword research, you know what the topics of the four videos will be. You can upload them all to YouTube and schedule them to be published on the correct day and time. Or you can edit one a week and upload once a week.

Publish it to go live on the same day of the week and the same time, please. The YouTube algorithm loves consistency. And this will save your bacon if you have to evacuate for a hurricane the day before you're supposed to record a video.

Batch filming allows you to film one day a month for just a couple of hours. I'd say that's worth it, wouldn't you?

YOUTUBER ACTION ITEM #7

Your final challenge is to think about which day will be your recording day and which will be your posting day.

You can record at night after the kids are in bed if you buy a few inexpensive studio lights. You can record on the weekends. You can record at home or at the office. You can record in your car while you're parked in the driveway—not while driving, please!

You can record vlog style where you're out and about in the community. I don't care when and where you film, as long as you do it.

Put it on your calendar, whether it's weekly, every two weeks, or monthly, and set an an alarm an hour or two ahead of time to remind you.

I started out weekly, and when I discovered batch filming, it made my life a hundred times easier, but most people don't start off that way. Simply make a promise to yourself that you will not blow it off.

Are you the type of person who makes promises you consistently fail to keep? No, I didn't think so. Because you will not earn the kind of income you want to earn if you can't be consistent.

So, choose a day and time to publish it on YouTube each week. Declare your day/time below:

————————————————————————————————

I give myself at least four days to get the video ready before posting. I edit out the mistakes, add some graphics and titles, some background music, and voila. I don't do crazy elaborate editing. You can if you want to, but it can be a real time suck.

I highly recommend outsourcing the editing as soon as you possibly can. Don't spend a whole week editing a video. It's not necessary unless you're marketing a $5,000,000 home. And in that case, hire a professional!

Your video needs to be visually interesting, but it should still allow you time to do what you do best—sell houses.

Pick a recording day/time and a publishing day/time. Put it on your calendar.

Pat yourself on the back. You're going to be a rock star!

CONCLUSION

*(also known as, more proof that
this stuff actually works!)*

Congratulations, YouTuber! I am so proud of you for doing this. Not only for doing the challenge but also for daring to be different! For daring to do something that other agents are too inhibited to do. Daring to generate business for yourself in a way that's enjoyable, cheap, and ridiculously effective. For daring to defy the old school mentality of lead gen strategy, even though your broker and your colleagues tell you you're wasting your time. (Show him my channel if he doesn't think it's possible to get business from YouTube—www.YouTube.com/KarinCarrRealEstate)

And I'm not going to lie. Becoming a bit of a celebrity is pretty sweet too!

My business took off dramatically when I committed to making weekly YouTube videos. Not only did I start making a helluva lot more money, my entire life changed.

I started getting so many leads and clients that I had to hire other agents to help me handle them all.

I began getting requests to speak at national real estate conferences. The Keller Williams corporate office asked me to do a live webinar on their education channel.

I even had a casting producer from a huge TV channel ask me to audition for a show they have in development. I didn't approach them—they approached me! All because of YouTube. (Say a little prayer for me that this works out, would you please?)

I've seen my students' businesses take off after committing to a YouTube strategy.

> *How long will it be before you start getting clients from YouTube? It's hard to say. I've had students that got leads in the first month or two. And I had one student finally get her first lead at the one year mark. She got frustrated with the lack of results but she kept going and had faith, tweaked her delivery and her graphics, got better at editing, reviewed her channel's analytics, tried new things, and was consistent week after week after week. Sometimes it takes longer than you think it will but you just keep going. Now THAT is commitment, people.*

How long it will take to see results really depends on so many things, like how big your market is, how much competition there is, how many searches are being done each month for the videos you're making, how well you have defined and attracted your niche, and how relatable you are in your videos.

> *But you will never know how effective your YouTube channel will be at bringing you new clients if you give up after a couple of months because you haven't seen results yet.*

I've seen countless posts in our private YouTube for Agents Students Only Facebook group like this:

Akbar AK Ali is 😊 feeling motivated.
June 27

Just wanted to share this email I got today. This was the second inquiry I got this week from YouTube. It's totally got me motivated to crank out more videos. Thank you Karin Atkinson Carr for sharing your knowledge and experience!!

Figure 8.1 Screenshot of a student's success shared in our Facebook group

Or this:

Figure 8.2 Screenshot of a student's success shared in our Facebook group

And this!

Figure 8.3 Screenshot of a student's success shared in our Facebook group

It is the highlight of my day when I see these posts! I jump up and down, I cheer, and I celebrate right along with my friends.

Would you like to get clients each and every month (or even week) from YouTube? You can, so now it's up to you.

Your channel looks fabulous, you have committed to an upload schedule and you will keep doing it until you see results, you know the secret sauce (keyword research), you will stop being a typical pushy salesperson in your videos like everyone else, and instead, you will give, give, give with no expectation of getting anything in return.

But you *will* get something in return. You'll have a career you can be proud of.

Go knock 'em dead, my friend. I'm cheering for you!

- Karin

Where do we go from here?

I f you are excited about your new YouTube journey and you feel prepared enough to start making great videos, please tag me on social @YouTubeforAgents so I can follow you and cheer you on!

I'm honored you took the time to read this book to the end and I'm thrilled that you like to geek out on video as much as I do. If you enjoyed it and would consider writing a review on Amazon, I would greatly appreciate it!

You can do so here: https://www.amazon.com/dp/B07WYQWDMT

Please join my Facebook group to network with other like-minded agents and get ideas for video topics, brainstorm about editing, and get constructive feedback on the videos you make. https://www.facebook.com/groups/YouTubeforrealestateagents/

We have a ton of fun in that group, so you should definitely join— all the cool kids are doing it.

You are also welcome to check out my agents-only YouTube channel where I share tips on making videos that get your phone to ring!

https://www.YouTube.com/KarinCarr

And if you want step by step instruction on the actual video creation process along with personal coaching from me, I invite you to join my program, YouTube for Agents. It's only open a few times a year so if it's not open now, sign up to get on the waiting list and I'll personally notify you when enrollment opens next.

YouTube for Agents is the absolute FASTEST way to learn how to dominate your market with video, establish yourself as a local expert, and get a steady stream of warm real estate leads calling YOU when they're ready to buy or sell.

The course is video based instruction (did you really expect anything else?) It's on-demand so you can go at your own pace, along with a private Facebook group where I do additional coaching and training.

You will learn things like:

The equipment / software you need
Setting up your YouTube account
What to say in your videos
Filming a video that gets prospects to call you
In-depth keyword research
Recording best practices
Editing basics (options for PC, Mac, or web-based)
Optimizing the video to get found in YouTube and Google searches
Promoting the video
Tons of technical resources
And so much more!

Find out more at: https://www.youtubeforagentscourse.com

But please, PLEASE, promise me that you will not stick this book on your shelf and never look at it again. If you want to change your business, you need to take massive action. YouTube has completely changed my life, and I know it can change yours too.

Happy filming!

RESOURCES AND BONUSES

These are things I've mentioned throughout the book that have helped me enormously on my YouTube journey. Some are affiliate links, some are not, and some are things I have created to help you get started.

Ideal Customer Avatar Worksheet http://youtubesuccesschecklist.com/ica/

Keywords Everywhere https://keywordseverywhere.com/

Tubebuddy (*) https://www.tubebuddy.com/friendsofkarin

LionDesk (*) http://www.LionDesk.com/#_a_5469

Leadpages(*)https://leadpages.pxf.io/c/1433947/466534/5673

Canva https://www.canva.com/

Easy Agent Pro websites(*) https://www.easyagentpro.com/signup/#_r_karin50

Channel Art Template in Canva
PLEASE NOTE: YOU MUST MAKE A COPY OF THIS DOCUMENT

BEFORE YOU START EDITING IT
http://youtubeforagents.site/channelart

Fiverr (*) http://www.fiverr.com/s2/a63803abb8

Blog post all about the gear I have used over the years http://youtubeforagents.site/gear

Virtual Assistant Job Board(*) http://store.onlinejobs.ph/?aid=188880

Georgia Coast Homes YouTube Channel www.Youtube.com/KarinCarrRealEstate

YouTube for Agents YouTube Channel www.Youtube.com/KarinCarr

YouTube Success Checklist https://www.youtubesuccesschecklist.com/freeleads/

ACKNOWLEGEMENTS

If you enjoyed this book, I would be eternally grateful if you took a minute to write a review. Reviews are to authors what comments, likes, and shares are to real estate agents on YouTube. So, please write a review if you found this book helpful.

You can write a review on Amazon here: https://www.amazon.com/dp/B07WYQWDMT

I want to especially thank the founding members of YouTube for Agents. You took a chance on me in March 2018 when my coaching program was just a crazy idea in the back of my mind and convinced me it was worth doing.

Your suggestions, feedback, guidance, and encouragement made me keep going to improve this program and make it the best it could be. I am so proud of what we have created together!

Hearing about your wins and successes brings me more joy than you'll ever know. Every single time you tell me me you got a new client from YouTube, I feel like a proud mama! I've learned that I love teaching more than I ever thought possible.

You, my students, have truly given me a whole new career that makes me jump out of bed each morning with a smile on my face. I will be forever indebted to you.

Made in the USA
Columbia, SC
12 September 2021